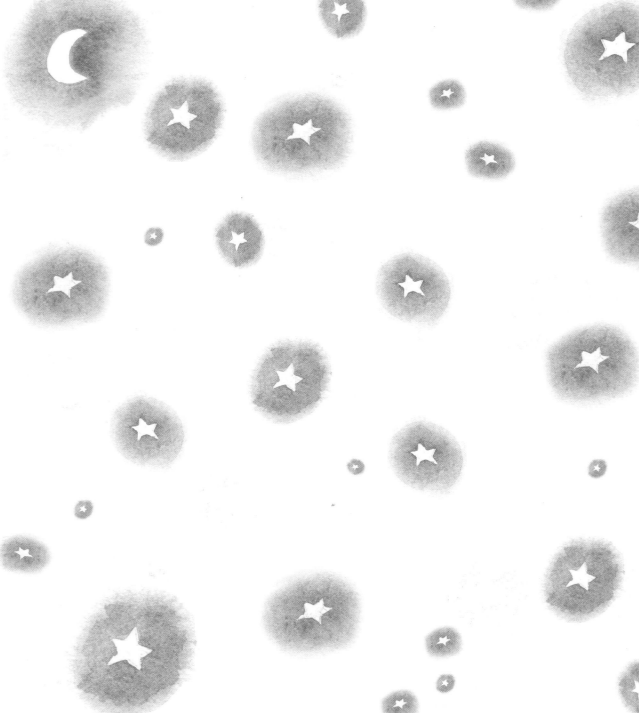

This edition published by Standard Publishing
8121 Hamilton Avenue, Cincinnati, OH 45231
A division of Standex International Corporation

First edition 2005
Copyright © 2005 AD Publishing Services Ltd
1 Churchgates, The Wilderness, Berkhamsted,
Herts HP4 2UB
Text copyright © 2005 AD Publishing Ltd,
Sally Ann Wright
Illustrations copyright © 2005 Honor Ayres
Editorial Director Annette Reynolds
Art Director Gerald Rogers
Pre-production Krystyna Hewitt
Production John Laister

Printed in Singapore

ISBN 0-7847-1776-1

11 10 09 08 07 06 05   9 8 7 6 5 4 3 2 1

This book belongs to

Liam Smith

A gift on the occasion of

Your Brother's
Baptism

with love from

LENNART HOLMQUIST
Jill Holmquist _Kristofer Holmquist_

date

October 18, 2009

A Child's
BIBLE

Sally Ann Wright
and
Honor Ayres

Contents

When the world began

Before anything else was made, God was there in the darkness.

God made light to shine in the darkness and saw that it was good.

God shaped the land so there were snow-topped mountains and deep blue seas.

God filled the land with flowering plants and fruit-bearing trees.

God made the hot sun to give light by day and the silvery moon and stars to light up the night sky.

God filled the sea with colorful creatures large and small and the air with buzzing bees and bright birds that sang.

God filled the earth with lumbering elephants and long=necked giraffes, with big cats covered in patterns and stripes, and with rhinos, antelope, deer, rabbits, and tiny mice. God made the first man and woman. They were called Adam and Eve.

God talked to Adam and Eve, and they talked to him. God wanted them to enjoy his world and be his friends.

God looked at the world he had made and saw that it was beautiful. Then God rested.

The whispering snake

God made a garden for Adam and Eve to live
in and asked them to take care of all
the animals. He told them they
could eat anything they
wanted except the fruit from
one tree.

But the snake came and
whispered to Eve. He showed her how good
the fruit on that one tree looked. Suddenly it
seemed better than all the other fruit God had
given them.

Eve took a big, deep bite. Then she shared it
with Adam.

Adam and Eve looked at each other. They felt
guilty. They realized that they had done the one
thing that God had told them not to do. They had
spoiled everything.

Now Adam and Eve were unhappy. And God was unhappy. They couldn't stay any longer in the garden God had made for them. They couldn't be his special friends any more.

Noah's floating zoo

God's beautiful world was spoiled. The people God had made could not live together happily. They did not share. They were not kind to each other. They were selfish, and they were greedy. They cared only about themselves.

They started to fight and hurt each other. They took things that belonged to others. They forgot about God and about how to love and care for other people.

God was sad. But there was one man who was good. Noah still loved God. He tried to love other people and care for his family and the world God had made.

God told Noah to build an ark, a big boat that would float on water.

Noah filled the ark with birds and animals of every kind. Soon there would be rain, and the rain would cause a flood that would wash the whole earth clean again.

When Noah, his family, and all the animals were safe inside the ark, the rain began to fall. It rained, and it rained, and it rained.

The rivers burst their banks, and the seas flooded the land. But Noah's ark floated on the water.

When the rain stopped and dry land at last appeared again, God told Noah and the animals they could leave the ark. A bright rainbow filled the sky.

Noah thanked God for keeping them safe. And God promised there would never be another flood like it.

Abraham moves house

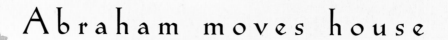

Many years after Noah, God chose a man called Abraham to be his friend.

God told Abraham to leave his home and take his family with him to a new land. God promised Abraham that he would give him a new home in a beautiful country, a big family, and everything he could want.

Abraham listened. He didn't know where he was going. He didn't know how long it would take. But Abraham trusted God. He and his wife, Sarah, packed their things.

They took their servants and their camels, their sheep and their goats, and set off on their journey, camping in tents along the way.

When they reached the land of Canaan, God told them this was their new home. And it was just as beautiful as God had promised.

A baby called laughter

Abraham and Sarah were happy in Canaan, but there was one thing missing. God had promised them a big family. Their goats had kids. Their sheep had lambs. Their camels had baby camels. But Abraham and Sarah still didn't have any children.

Abraham looked up at the stars in the night sky.

"Don't worry," he heard God say. "You will have children. One day your family will be as many as the stars you can see above you!"

Weeks passed. Months passed. Years passed. Abraham and Sarah thought that they were now too old to have children.

But still Abraham trusted God. And then Sarah had a lovely baby boy. They were so happy. They named him Isaac, which means "laughter."

Abraham looked again at the stars and smiled. God had kept his promise.

Jacob tricks his brother

Abraham's grandsons, Esau and Jacob, were twins.

Esau was born first. He was the favorite of his father Isaac. Jacob was born second. He was the favorite of his mother Rebekah.

Isaac grew to be an old man, and the time came when he thought he must bless his eldest son before he died. He asked Esau to go hunting and prepare for him a tasty meal.

But Rebekah wanted Jacob to have the blessing. It would mean Jacob would be head of the family when Isaac died.

Rebekah dressed Jacob in Esau's clothes and wrapped animal skins around his arms and neck, so that he felt hairy like his brother. Then she prepared a tasty meal for Isaac to eat.

Jacob went to his father with the food. Isaac's eyes were weak, and he couldn't see his son, but he felt his hairy skin. When Isaac asked him who he was, Jacob lied to his father. So Isaac believed that Jacob was Esau. And Isaac gave his special blessing to Jacob instead of to his eldest son.

Later, when Esau came home, he went to his father for the blessing. Then Isaac realized his mistake, and Esau went looking for his younger brother who had tricked him! Esau was so angry that Jacob was frightened of what Esau might do.

His mother told Jacob to run away and stay with his uncle Laban. So Jacob left and made his home with his uncle until after his father had died. While he was there, Jacob fell in love with Laban's younger daughter, Rachel, and married her.

Joseph, the favorite son

Jacob loved his wife Rachel very much. But he had three other wives too, a big family of twelve sons, and a daughter. His favorite child was Joseph.

When Joseph was seventeen, Jacob gave him a beautiful, brightly colored coat. This made Joseph's brothers jealous. They wished Jacob loved them as much as he loved Joseph.

Then one day they found a way to get rid of Joseph. While out taking care of their father's sheep, they sold Joseph to some traders who were on their way to Egypt!

If that were not enough, they took his beautiful coat and dipped it in goat's blood. Then they returned to their father, pretending to be sad. They showed him the coat and the blood — and poor Jacob thought that his favorite son had been killed by a wild animal!

But God had plans for Joseph.

A very happy family

God looked after Joseph while he was in Egypt.
     When the king had strange dreams that kept him
awake at night, Joseph was brought to help him
understand what they meant. Through those dreams God

showed Joseph how he could help himself and all the people of Egypt.

For seven years there would be good harvests and plenty of food for everyone. But then there would be seven years that no food would grow. The king made sure that Joseph was in charge so that food could be saved and shared so that no one would go hungry.

It worked so well that Joseph's brothers in Canaan came to Egypt for food. What a surprise they had when they discovered that their little brother was there to help them! Jacob was overjoyed to find his son was still alive, and the whole family came to live in the land of Egypt.

Miriam and the princess

Kings came and went, and soon the Egyptians forgot how Joseph had helped them.

God's people were made to be slaves. They had to work hard for the king. And when baby boys were born, soldiers came to take them away from their mothers.

When Jochebed's baby son was born, she decided to hide him. At first it was easy, but soon he made too much noise. Then Jochebed had a clever plan.

She put her baby in a waterproof basket and hid him in the reeds by the River Nile. She told her daughter Miriam to watch and wait.

An Egyptian princess came to the river and saw the basket. When she found the baby boy inside, she knew she wanted to keep him.

"I will call him Moses," she said.

Miriam was delighted! She told the princess that she knew a woman who would look after the baby until he was big enough to live in the palace. And Miriam went to get her mother!

Flies, boils, and locusts

When Moses grew up to be a man, God spoke to him from a bush burning in the desert.

"Go to the king of Egypt," said God. "Tell him to let my people go!"

Moses was afraid. He didn't want to go to the king! So God told him to take his brother Aaron with him to help.

Moses and Aaron went to give the king God's message. But the king was angry. He wouldn't let the people go. Instead he told the slave drivers to make them work even harder!

So God sent ten terrible plagues on the people of Egypt.

First the river Nile was turned as red as blood. Then there were frogs, everywhere there were frogs — in the houses, the food, and the beds! Then the air was full of

33

gnats, itching and biting; then buzzing flies. All the horses, donkeys, camels, cattle, sheep, and goats became ill and died. Then the people were covered with nasty black boils. They were so sore that they couldn't stand up. And there was a terrible hailstorm that destroyed all the new crops and stripped the leaves from the trees. Locusts came later and ate anything and everything that had been left. Then the land was quiet and covered in complete darkness for three days.

God kept his people safe during this time. And when each plague happened, the king of Egypt agreed to let God's people go. But as soon as the plague was over, the king changed his mind.

Finally the tenth and most terrible of all the plagues came on the people of Egypt. God told Moses to get the people ready to leave. They put a special sign on their doors, packed their bags, and put on their cloaks and shoes. They they ate a final meal of roast lamb with herbs.

That night every first-born male animal and every first-born son in Egypt died, including the king's son.

The king of Egypt sent for Moses.

"Take God's people and go!" he shouted.

Escape from Egypt

The Israelites took their sheep and goats and went as quickly as they could. But they had not gone far when the king changed his mind again.

"Bring them back!" he shouted.

The Israelites stood with the Red Sea in front of them and the Egyptian chariots behind them. They were trapped.

"Don't be afraid," said Moses. "God has brought us this far. He will look after us now."

Moses stretched out his hand across the water. A strong wind blew and made a pathway for them to cross over to the other side of the sea.

When the Egyptians tried to follow, Moses stretched out his hand again. The waters returned and the chariots got stuck in the mud. God had saved his people!

Ten rules for life

God looked after his people as they wandered in the desert. He also gave Moses rules so his people could live the way he wanted them to.

''I am the Lord your God,
who rescued you when you were slaves in Egypt.
Don't talk to any other gods instead of me.
Don't pray to statues,
pictures of the earth, sky or sea, instead of me.
Think about how you use my name.

Do not swear or use my name carelessly.
Remember the day of rest I give you
and keep it special.
Love your mother and father
and listen to what they say.
Do not plot to kill anyone.
Be faithful to your husband or wife.
Do not steal.
Do not tell lies about other people.
Don't look greedily
at things that belong to other people.''

The walls of Jericho

After many years in the desert, Moses died and God asked Joshua to take his people into Canaan, the beautiful land he had promised them.

But first they had to get past the strong, high walls of the city of Jericho. The people there were fierce and unfriendly, and there was no other way through the city.

Joshua listened, and God told him what to do.

The people had to march around the walls of the city for six days behind the priests, who carried the special box containing God's laws. The priests blew loudly on their trumpets, and the people inside the city of Jericho looked on, amazed.

On the seventh day, they marched around the city not once, not twice, but seven times! Then the priests blew on their trumpets . . . and all the people shouted . . . and the walls of Jericho came tumbling down to the ground!

Gideon's prayer

God's people had not been long in the land of Canaan when they started to worship the gods of the people around them. They forgot how God had helped them in the past, and they did not keep his rules.

Then the Midianite armies started to attack them. They rode in on camels, stole all their crops, and stripped the land bare. After seven years of this, God's people were very hungry, and they cried to him for help.

God answered their prayer. God sent his angel to Gideon and told him he would rescue the people from the Midianites.

Now Gideon was afraid. He was not a brave soldier. He was not even a brave man. When the angel came, he was hiding in a wine press, beating out what little wheat he had been able to keep from the enemy.

But Gideon listened to God.

First he pulled down the altar to the false god, Baal, and made an altar to the God of his people. Then when the Midianites next prepared to attack, Gideon called his people together to fight. But before they went into battle, Gideon prayed.

That night he put out a woollen fleece on the ground. The next morning the fleece was wet with dew, while the ground around it was dry. Then Gideon prayed again.

The following night he put out the woollen fleece again. The next morning the fleece was dry, while the ground around it was wet with dew.

Gideon had asked God to show him that he would be with his people and not let them lose the battle. He had asked God to make the fleece wet on the first night, then dry on the second night,

even though the ground around it was not. God had answered Gideon's prayer. Gideon was now ready to do whatever God asked of him.

So just as God had told him, Gideon went to the Midianite camp by night with only 300 soldiers. And God gave them the victory!

The boy who listened to God

Hannah had wanted a baby for a long time. When she gave birth to baby Samuel, she was so happy that she promised that Samuel would serve God all his life. So when Samuel was old enough, he went to learn how to serve God with Eli, the priest.

One night when he was sleeping, Samuel heard someone call his name. Samuel jumped up and went to Eli's room.

"Here I am," he said. "You called me."

"No, I didn't," said Eli. "Go back to sleep."

Samuel lay down and tried to sleep again. Again he heard someone call his name and went to Eli.

"Go back to sleep," said Eli. "I didn't call you."

Then Samuel heard the voice a third time, and went to Eli. This time Eli knew who it was.

"God wants to speak to you," Eli said. "If you hear him again, say, 'Speak to me, Lord. I'm listening.'"

So Samuel answered God when he spoke again, and he listened to what God said.

Samuel became a wise leader and helped the people of God obey him.

David fights a giant

David was his father's youngest son. He looked after the sheep, and protected them from lions and bears.

One day David went to see his brothers who were soldiers in King Saul's army.

They watched each day as Goliath, the Philistine champion, marched up and down and taunted them.

"Who will dare to fight me?" he roared.

No one dared!

No one stepped forward. Goliath was a giant of a man, and they were all afraid — all except David.

David was too small to wear the king's armor, but he was brave enough to fight.

"God helped me against the lions and bears," he said. "God will help me now."

David took five smooth pebbles from the stream and faced the giant.

He put one pebble in his sling and whirled it around his head. The stone hit Goliath on the forehead and killed him — and the Philistine army ran away! King Saul's army cheered! God had helped David win the battle.

The shepherd's song

Imagine you are a lamb, playing in a big field.

God is like the loving shepherd who looks after you.

God makes sure you have everything you need.

He finds green fields where you can rest.

He leads you to quiet streams where you can drink.

He guides you along safe paths.

Even when the path is rocky and slippery,

if you fall into danger, God will still help you to safety.

You don't need to be frightened.

God's love and kindness will always be with you,

all the days of your life.

You will always be with God,

and God will always be with you.

Solomon's special gift

David ruled as king after Saul, and when David died, his son Solomon became king.

One night God came to Solomon in a dream and asked him what special gift he would like God to give him.

"You have already shown such love to my father David and to me," said Solomon. "All I need is the wisdom to choose between what is good and evil as I rule your people."

God was pleased with Solomon. So God gave him the wisdom he asked for, but God also gave him great wealth and made the people love him.

Then one day two women came to Solomon to ask him to judge between them.

They had each had a baby boy in the same house. One baby died during the night. His mother stole the living baby and put the dead baby in the other woman's arms. In the morning the other woman realized that her baby had been taken away, but the other woman said the living baby was hers.

Solomon knew how to find out who the real mother was. He asked for the baby to be cut in half and one half to be given to each of the mothers.

"No!" said the real mother. "Give her the baby, but do not kill him."

So Solomon knew that this was the real mother because she loved her son too much to let him die.

All God's people heard of Solomon's wise judgement and saw how God had blessed him.

God looks after Elijah

In the land of Israel, the rivers were dry and the fields were dry. There was nothing to eat and nothing to drink. It had not rained for a long time.

But Elijah knew that God would look after him.

God told Elijah where to find a stream where he could drink the fresh water. God told the ravens to bring food for Elijah. Then the stream dried up.

But Elijah knew that God would look after him.

God told Elijah where to find a woman who would share her food with him. The woman used her last bowl of flour and her last drop of oil to bake some bread. She shared the bread with Elijah and her son.

When the woman looked again, her bowl was full of flour and her jar was full of oil! For as long as she shared what she had, God made sure that she and her son and Elijah would never be hungry.

The little servant girl

Naaman was a brave soldier, but he had a horrible skin disease. Nobody wanted to go near him in case they became ill too.

His wife had a little Israelite servant girl. She liked her master and wanted to help him.

"If he would go to see the prophet Elisha," she told her mistress, "God could make Naaman better." So Naaman went to Israel to find Elisha.

When Naaman arrived, Elisha knew why he had come. He sent his servant out with a message to go and wash seven times in the River Jordan.

At first Naaman was angry. Why would Elisha not come and make him well himself? But one of his servants encouraged him to go to the River Jordan.

So Naaman went and washed seven times. When he came out of the water, his skin was clear again!

Naaman was amazed!

"Now I know," he said, "that here in Israel is the only true God in all the world."

The one true God

Daniel and his friends, Shadrach, Meshach and
Abednego, had lived in Babylon for a long time. They
had been taken away from their homes and families and
been made to work for King Nebuchadnezzar.

One day the king decided to make a huge golden
statue. He invited all the important people of his kingdom
to come and see it. Then he gave an order that they should
bow down and worship the statue when they heard the
music play. Anyone who refused to bow down would be
thrown into a fiery furnace.

When the music started to play, everyone bowed
down low to worship the statue — everyone except
Shadrach, Meshach and Abednego.

The three men were brought before the angry king.

"You have one more chance!" he said to them. "Worship my statue or you will die!"

"We may die, King Nebuchadnezzar," they answered, "or our God may save us. But we cannot worship anyone but him."

The king was so angry that he had the furnace heated seven times more, and the men were thrown into it with their hands tied.

But as the king watched, he grew amazed, for he saw not three, but four men inside the furnace, walking freely about. One of them seemed like an angel. The king ordered them to come out. He saw that no part of them was burned. He realized that they didn't even smell of smoke! Then the king knew how great their God was. He gave the men the best jobs in his kingdom.

The lions' den

Daniel loved God and knew that he should work hard and always be honest. So King Darius of Babylon gave him an important job in his court.

But this made other men in Babylon jealous. So they went to King Darius and asked him to make a new law. No one should be worshipped but the king alone — or they would be thrown into a den of lions!

The king thought it was a good law, and he made it. But Daniel knew that he should worship only the one true God. So he worshipped God — just as he had always done — and the men told the king.

Daniel was taken to the lions' den and thrown inside. And the king could not sleep that night.

In the morning King Darius went to the lions' den. He couldn't believe it when he heard Daniel's voice.

"I am here, my King!" Daniel said. "God sent an

angel to close the lions' mouths!"

Then King Darius made a new law. "Daniel's God is a great God," he said. "From now on everyone must worship Daniel's God!"

Jonah runs away

Jonah loved God and listened to what he said. But one day God asked Jonah to go to the people in Nineveh.

"Tell them they are doing very bad things," said God. "Tell them to stop and be sorry, and then I will forgive them."

Jonah didn't want to! Instead he got on a ship going in the other direction and ran away!

But soon a storm blew up. The wind blew, the waves splashed onto the deck, and everyone was afraid they would drown.

Jonah quickly realized that the storm was his fault.
"Throw me into the sea!" he said. "Then the storm will
stop, and you will be safe."

The sailors didn't want to hurt Jonah, but they were
afraid, so they threw Jonah into the sea. The wind
dropped, the waves stopped splashing, and God sent a
huge fish to swallow Jonah.

Jonah sat and thought inside the body of the big fish for three days and three nights. Then he prayed to God.

"I'm sorry!" he said to God. "I will do as you ask."

The fish swam near the shore and spat Jonah onto the sandy beach.

"Go to Nineveh," said God. And this time Jonah obeyed God.

Jonah told the people in Nineveh that God wanted them to stop doing bad things. The people listened and were sorry. And because God loved them, he was happy and forgave them.

A baby born in Bethlehem

Mary was going to have a baby. An angel had told her he would be very special and he was to be called Jesus.

Just before the baby was due, she and Joseph travelled to Bethlehem to be counted by the Roman soldiers. There were so many people there that the only place to sleep was a stable. When Mary's baby was born, she wrapped him up and placed him in the manger.

Soon afterward shepherds came and found them! Angels had appeared to them in the night sky and told them God's own son had been born. They knew they had found the right baby because there he was — asleep in a manger!

Gifts for the baby king

When Jesus was born, a new star appeared in the sky. Wise men in the east saw it. They believed that it meant that a baby king had been born.

The wise men set off to find the baby king, following the star. When they reached Jerusalem, they asked King Herod if the baby king was there.

King Herod was angry! He was the only king in the land! But he sent the wise men to Bethlehem to see if they could find the baby king there.

The wise men followed the star until they found a little house. Inside the house they found Mary with Jesus, her little son.

The wise men offered Jesus gifts of gold, frankincense, and myrrh. Then they returned to their own land again.

John baptizes Jesus

When Mary was expecting baby Jesus, her cousin Elizabeth was about to have a baby boy too. Elizabeth's baby was called John.

Now both John and Jesus had grown up to be men. John grew up listening to what God said to him. He knew that soon Jesus would come with God's power to help them all know God better.

John baptized people who came to him because they were sorry for the wrong things they had done. One day Jesus came to the River Jordan and asked to be baptized.

"I can't baptize you!" John told him. "I am not important enough!"

But Jesus told him it was what God wanted him to do. So John baptized Jesus in the river.

God was pleased with Jesus. The people who were watching heard God's voice and saw the Holy Spirit

come to Jesus to give him the power he
needed to work for God, his Father.

Jesus makes special friends

Jesus started to teach people about God, his Father, near Lake Galilee.

He wanted some friends to be with him as he travelled. So he chose twelve from the people around him.

Two of them were brothers working hard, trying to catch fish from their boat. Two more were mending their fishing nets.

"Peter! Andrew!" Jesus called. "James and John! Leave your fishing and come with me! Come and learn more about God!"

The four fishermen left everything behind. They knew Jesus was special and wanted to follow him.

Jesus chose Matthew who collected money for the Romans. Other people didn't like tax collectors, but Jesus said anyone who wanted to could be his friend.

He chose Philip and Bartholomew, Thomas and

James, Simon and two men who were called Judas. All of these were his special friends. They listened to him teach and were with him as he cared for all the people who came to him for help.

God's blessing

God blesses people who love him with their whole hearts —
they belong to God.

God blesses people who are very sad — he will put
his arms around them.

God blesses people who don't show off to
others — he will give them the whole earth.

God blesses people who try to do as he says —
they will be given all they could ever want.

God blesses people who are kind to others —
he will be kind to them.

God blesses people who think good thoughts
about others — they will see God!

God blesses people who help others to make friends
again — they will be called his children.

A prayer Jesus taught his friends

Our Father in heaven,
    holy is your name.
Your kingdom come,
    your will be done on earth,
    as it is in Heaven.
Give us today the food
    we need,
    and forgive us when we
    do bad things,
    just as we should forgive
    those who are unkind to us.
Help us not to think or do things that
    hurt other people,
    but keep us safe and close to you
    always.

The hole in the roof

There was once a man who could not walk. When his friends heard that Jesus was in their town, they carried him on his mat to see Jesus. They thought that Jesus might be able to help him.

But everyone wanted to see Jesus! When they got to the house where Jesus was, there was no room for them to get through the door.

Carefully they carried the man up the steps outside and then started to make a hole in the roof. When the hole was big enough, they lowered their friend down — right in front of Jesus and the crowd of people.

Jesus saw how much the friends cared about the man on the mat. He saw how much the man wanted to walk.

"Stand up, pick up your mat, and walk," Jesus said.

The man stood up. The man picked up his mat. The man walked home! Everyone was amazed. And his friends couldn't have been happier!

The storm on the lake

Jesus often told people about how much God loved them. He showed them how to care about other people.

After one very tiring day, Jesus sailed across Lake Galilee with his friends. He put his head down on a cushion and quickly fell asleep.

Suddenly the wind blew stronger and lightning flashed across the sky. Jesus' friends heard the crack of thunder and felt the boat rock back and forth dangerously.

"Help us, Jesus!" they shouted. But Jesus was still asleep.

"Help us, or we'll drown!" they shouted again.

This time Jesus woke up. He spoke to the wind and the waves.

"Peace! Be still!"

The wind dropped. The water became still again. Jesus' friends were amazed. Jesus had calmed the storm.

Jesus heals a little girl

One day a church leader named Jairus came to Jesus as he walked through the streets. He fell to his knees and begged Jesus for help.

"Please come to my house!" he said. "My only daughter is very ill."

Jairus' daughter was twelve=years=old. But as Jesus tried to make his way to Jairus' house, people pushed against him. Other people wanted his help too.

Then someone from Jairus' house ran up to him.

"It's too late," he said. "Your daughter has died!"

"Don't worry," said Jesus to Jairus. "Trust me and your little girl will be healed."

Jesus went into the house with three of his friends. He took the girl by the hand and said, "Get up, little girl!"

The girl sat up, very much alive!

"Now give her something to eat," said Jesus.

Jesus had brought her back to life.

Bread and fish

Wherever Jesus went, crowds of people followed him. One day when the people had followed him out of the town, Jesus saw that everyone was hungry. He asked his friend Philip how they could find food for everyone.

"For all these people?" Philip asked. "We don't have enough money to buy food for everyone here!"

But then Andrew came to Jesus.

"This little boy has five small loaves and two little fish," he said. "He says he wants to share it with Jesus."

Jesus smiled. He told his friends to get all the people to sit down. There were over 5,000 people there — men, women, and children.

Jesus took the bread and the little fish from the boy. He asked God to bless them. Then he shared the food with his friends. His friends shared the food with all the people sitting down . . . and they shared it with each other. Everyone sat and ate the food until they had had enough. Then Jesus' friends collected up everything that was left into twelve baskets.

It was a miracle! All the people had enough to eat, and there was still food left over!

A real friend

Jesus told this story so people knew how they could make God happy.

"There was once a man who was walking from Jerusalem to Jericho. He was attacked by robbers who left him lying hurt by the side of the road.

"A priest came along. He saw the injured man, but ignored him. He walked past on the other side.

"A Levite followed the priest. He looked at the injured man, but walked on without helping him.

"At last a man from another country, a Samaritan, came by. He stopped and bandaged the man's wounds. He put the man on his donkey and took him to an inn, where he gave the innkeeper money to look after the injured man."

"If you want to make God happy," said Jesus, "care for other people just as the Samaritan did."

The lost sheep

Jesus once told this story.

"Once there was a shepherd with one hundred sheep. He named each of them and knew how each one was different from the others.

"One day he found that a sheep was missing. Quickly the shepherd made sure that the other ninety-nine were safe, then he went to look for the lost sheep.

"The shepherd looked in ditches and muddy streams; he looked in brambles and on rocky ledges. The shepherd did not give up.

"Then the shepherd heard the sound of a sheep crying out to him. He picked up the little sheep, put it on his shoulders, and carried it home. He was so happy to have found his sheep that he threw a party."

"God is like that shepherd," said Jesus. "He is not happy unless everyone is safely in his care."

The loving father

Jesus told another story about a man who had two sons.

"One day the younger son went to his father and said that he wanted to leave home.

"'Give me my share of the money I should receive when you die, Father. I want to travel and explore the world.'"

"The father loved his son very much and was sad that he wanted to go. But he gave his son the money, and his son left home. He made lots of friends, and they helped him spend his money. But after a while, the money was all gone. When he had nothing left, his friends left him too. He was sad and lonely — and hungry! He had to get a job, and the only one he could get was feeding pigs, and

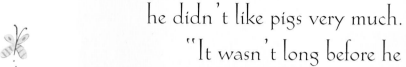

he didn't like pigs very much.

"It wasn't long before he realized how silly he was. Even the servants on his father's farm had more to eat than he did.

'"I will tell Dad how sorry I am and ask him if I can work on the farm as his servant,' he thought.'

"So he started the journey back. He was tired and dirty, and his clothes were in rags. But as he came near to his father's farm, he saw a man standing, watching, and waiting. As he drew closer, he saw that it was his father. His father had been waiting for him, hoping he would come home.

"As he started to say how sorry he was, his father threw his arms around him, with tears in his eyes.

'"You are home and that's all that matters,' said his father. He told his servants to get his son a new robe and to put a ring on his finger. His son had been lost but now he was found. And they had a party to celebrate!"

"God is like that father," said Jesus. "He watches and waits for us to say sorry when we do things that are wrong, and he is ready to forgive us when we come back to him."

The man who said thank you

There were many people in the time of Jesus who suffered from a horrible disease called leprosy.

Although they were very ill, people were afraid to help them because they thought they would catch the illness too. So those with leprosy lived outside the villages. People would throw stones at them if they came near.

One day as Jesus came into a village, he saw ten people with leprosy waiting for him. They called out to him for help. Jesus saw how much they needed to be healed and told them they could go and live normal lives again — he had made them well!

One of the ten who came from Samaria, was so happy that he came to Jesus and fell to his knees. He wanted to thank Jesus for healing him.

Jesus was kind to the Samaritan, but he was also sad. The other nine had gone; only one had come back to say thank you.

The man who could not see

Bartimaeus could not see. Because he could not see, he could not work. And because he could not work, he had nothing to eat. So Bartimaeus sat by the side of the road and held out his begging bowl, hoping people would be kind to him as they walked by.

One day Bartimaeus heard a crowd of people coming near. He could tell someone special was with them. Then he heard someone say that it was Jesus!

Bartimaeus had heard all about Jesus. He knew that Jesus cared about people. And he also knew that Jesus had healed people like him who were blind.

"Jesus! Help me!" Bartimaeus shouted out. The crowd told him to be quiet; Jesus was busy. But Bartimaeus called out even louder!

"Jesus! Please help me!"

Jesus stopped and asked Bartimaeus to come to him. "How can I help you?" Jesus asked.

"I want to see!" Bartimaeus said. So Jesus told him that because he believed, he would be able to see. And Bartimaeus could see from that moment on. Bartimaeus was so happy that he followed Jesus with the rest of the crowd.

A very little man

In Jericho there lived a man called Zacchaeus. He was rich, but he was lonely. He had no friends because he cheated the people around him by collecting too much money in taxes.

One day Jesus came to Jericho where Zacchaeus lived. Zacchaeus wanted to see Jesus, but he was not tall enough! So he climbed up a tree!

When Jesus reached the tree, he stopped and looked up.

"Come down, Zacchaeus!" said Jesus. "I want to come to your house and visit you."

Zacchaeus clambered down the tree in excitement.

"You are welcome to stay with me, Jesus!" he cried. After being with Jesus a short while, Zacchaeus was a changed man.

"I'm going to give half of all that I have to people who are poor! And if I have cheated anyone, I will pay him back four times as much."

Jesus smiled at Zacchaeus. "Today you have become God's friend!" Jesus said.

Jesus rides a donkey

The time had come for Jesus to go to Jerusalem for the Passover Feast for the last time.

Jesus sent two of his friends into a village where he knew a donkey and her colt were waiting for him. His friends brought back the animals and spread cloaks on the colt so Jesus could ride into Jerusalem on it.

People were waiting for him as he rode in. Crowds were following him, and others were leading the way. Some spread their cloaks as well as palms on the ground in front of Jesus. They waved palm branches and cheered.

"Here comes Jesus! Hooray for Jesus the king!"

Jerusalem was full of people. They turned and stared at Jesus riding on a donkey's colt.

The woman who gave everything

Jesus and his friends were in the temple courts while all kinds of people came to give gifts of money to God.

Many came and counted out gleaming gold coins. They were very rich.

But Jesus watched as a poor woman gave two small copper coins. It wasn't very much money, but it was everything she had.

"Did you see that poor woman?" Jesus asked his friends. "She has given the greatest gift of all to God. The others gave much but they still had plenty left for themselves. But this woman gave everything she had to God. God will look after her."

Love one another

When it was time to eat the Passover supper, Jesus went with his friends to an upstairs room in a house in the city of Jerusalem.

Their feet were hot and dusty and needed to be washed before the friends sat down to eat. Jesus found a towel and a bowl of water, but Peter didn't want Jesus to wash his feet. Jesus was their friend — not their servant.

So Jesus explained that when people love each other, they will do anything for each other. Jesus was happy to wash their feet because he loved his friends. He wanted them to love each other by showing they cared in whatever way they could.

Then Jesus told his friends that this would be the last time he ate with them before he died.

The soldiers in the garden

Judas had eaten the Passover supper with Jesus, but Judas was no longer Jesus' friend. Judas crept out of the room and went to betray Jesus to his enemies.

Jesus went with the others in the moonlight to an olive grove nearby. Here he took Peter, James, and John with him and asked them to keep watch while he prayed. But each time Jesus returned, they were asleep.

Jesus asked God to help him. Jesus knew that soon he would be left by all his friends to face his enemies alone.

Then through the darkness came flaming torches and the chinking of swords. Judas led the soldiers to Jesus and they arrested him. The other eleven friends panicked and ran away, leaving Jesus with the soldiers.

Jesus dies on a cross

That night Peter watched from a distance as Jesus was taken from place to place and his enemies tried to find something to accuse him of doing wrong.

The next day Jesus' enemies made Jesus carry a huge piece of wood to a place outside the city walls, and they crucified him with two criminals.

John watched and waited with Jesus' mother, Mary, and many of his friends. After many hours the sky turned black, and Jesus cried out, ''It is finished!'' before he died on the cross.

One of Jesus' friends, a man called Joseph, then came and took Jesus from the cross and put his body in the tomb he had bought for himself. A huge heavy stone was rolled across the entrance.

Mary weeps for Jesus

It was Sunday morning. Mary and two other women had come with spices to the place where they had buried their friend Jesus.

But what had happened? The huge round stone had been rolled away! The tomb was empty! Mary began to sob because Jesus' body was missing. But then the women saw two angels.

"Why are you crying?" the angels asked. "Do not be afraid," the angels told the women. "Jesus has been raised from the dead! Go quickly and tell his friends!"

As the women turned to leave, Mary heard someone else say her name. She knew that voice. Mary turned around. It was Jesus!

"Go and tell my friends that I am alive," said Jesus.
"I have seen Jesus!" Mary told the friends joyfully.
"Jesus is alive!"

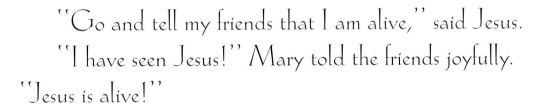

Jesus is alive!

Thomas was a twin. He knew how easy it was to mistake one person for another! Mary and all of Thomas' friends said Jesus was alive. But because Thomas hadn't seen Jesus since he died on the cross, Thomas couldn't be sure.

A week later all Jesus' friends met together in a locked room. Then Jesus appeared with them in the room! He turned to speak to Thomas.

"Come, Thomas," Jesus said. "Touch my hands. Come and see that I am Jesus, and I am alive, not dead!"

Then Thomas knew that it really was Jesus, alive and well again. Thomas didn't understand how these things happened. But he did believe!

Thomas got down on his knees.

"My Lord and my God!" he said.

Breakfast by the lake

Hundreds of people saw Jesus after he rose from the dead. He met his friends many times, but they never knew when or where they would see him.

One evening some of Jesus' friends went out fishing.

They stayed out all night, but by morning they had still caught nothing.

As the sun rose, they sailed back to the shore, and heard a man shouting to them.

"Have you caught anything?" he asked.

"Not a single fish!" they replied.

"Try throwing your nets on the right hand side of the boat," said the man.

When they did, they were amazed. Their net was bursting with fish! Then Peter realized who the man was: it was Jesus!

Peter jumped into the water and started to swim to the shore, leaving the others to pull in the catch. Jesus was cooking fish and warming some bread over a fire, and they all sat and had breakfast with him.

Then Jesus asked Peter if he loved him enough to do a special job for him. Jesus wanted Peter to teach other people about him and be their leader after he had returned to be with his father in Heaven.

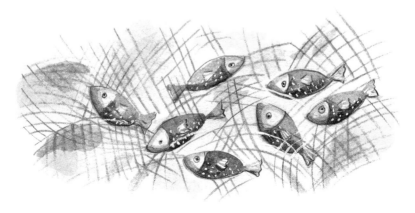

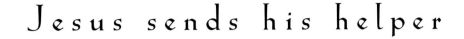

Jesus sends his helper

About forty days after Jesus had died and risen from the dead, he went to be with God once more. Jesus had promised that he would send his Holy Spirit to help his friends serve God and give them the power they needed to help other people. He had promised that he would never leave them again.

When Jesus' friends came together to celebrate the festival of Pentecost in Jerusalem, the Holy Spirit came to them. They heard a sound like the wind. They saw what looked like flames of fire. But instead of being afraid, suddenly they knew that they could do anything God wanted them to do. They knew that he was there to help them.

Peter talks about Jesus

When the Holy Spirit came, Jesus' friends started to tell people all about him. They were given the power to speak to the many people around them in different languages, so that everyone could understand what they said.

Soon Peter found there was a huge crowd listening to him. He explained how he, Peter the fisherman, was a changed man because the Holy Spirit had come. Then he told the people how much they needed God's help too.

"If you tell God you are sorry for the wrong things you have done," said Peter, "and trust Jesus who died and was alive again, then you can be God's friend."

More than 3,000 people became friends of Jesus that day. They shared everything they had and learned to care for each other as Jesus had taught them.

The man at the gate

One day Peter and John
went to pray in the Temple.
 They were met at the gate
by a man who couldn't walk.
He was brought there day
after day, so that he could sit
and beg for coins from the people who
went in the temple.

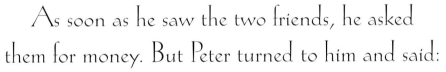

 As soon as he saw the two friends, he asked
them for money. But Peter turned to him and said:
 "I can't give you any money; I don't have any
to give! But Jesus has given me the power to give
you something much better. Stand up and walk!"
 Peter took him by the hand — and the man stood
up and walked, and then he jumped and ran about
telling everyone how great God was for making him
well again!

The death of Stephen

Soon many people came to know about Jesus. Some of these people became his followers and were known as Christians. But the new Christians had enemies just as Jesus had had enemies.

Stephen was one of Jesus' followers. He taught people about all the wonderful things Jesus had said and done. And like Peter, Stephen had Jesus' power to help other people and make them well. But Stephen was taken outside the city and killed for trying to teach others about Jesus.

Saul was one of the enemies. He stood by and watched — happy that anyone who called himself a Christian should die. Afterward Saul started to search for all those who followed the teaching of Jesus, and he had them thrown into prison.

The blinding light

Saul decided to go to Damascus to look for Christians there who should be put in prison.

Saul was nearly there when there was a blinding light all around him. He fell to his knees and heard a voice.

"Saul," said the voice, "why do you hurt me?"

"Who are you, Lord?" Saul asked.

"I am Jesus," the voice replied. "I have a job for you to do. Go into the city and someone will come and tell you what it is."

Saul was amazed — he had heard Jesus speaking to him!

Saul's friends were amazed — they heard a sound that seemed to come from nowhere!

But Saul found he could not see, so his friends had to lead him to Damascus.

Saul rides in a basket

The next three days were very strange for Saul. He could not see; he did not eat or drink; he was in a strange place with people he did not know.

But it was also strange for a Christian called Ananias. Jesus spoke to him too.

"Go to Straight Street, Ananias, and ask for Saul of Tarsus. I have sent him a vision in which you touch his eyes so that he can see again."

Ananias had heard about Saul and was afraid of him! But Jesus told him that he had special plans for Saul: he would be the person who would bring the good news about Jesus to thousands of people who hadn't heard about him.

So Ananias went to Saul and touched him. Immediately Saul was able to see again. The Holy Spirit came to Saul, and he was baptized.

Then Saul's life was completely changed. Before he met Jesus, he tried to stop the new Christians from sharing Jesus' love with others. Now he was a Christian and no one could stop him from telling other people about Jesus! But people did try to stop him. Soon Saul found that the Jewish leaders were plotting to kill him, and his new friends had to lower him in a basket down through a window in the city walls, so he could escape to Jerusalem.

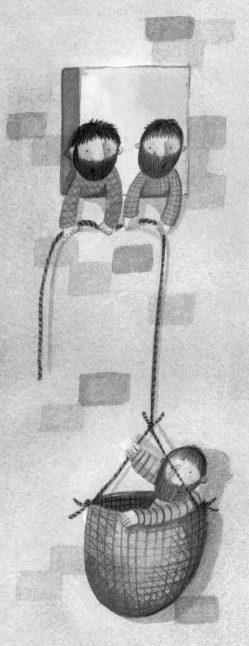

Peter and the angel

Over the next few years, many people came to know about Jesus. But Jesus' followers lived in danger.

Peter was put in prison. He was chained to two soldiers so he couldn't escape. Peter's friends prayed that God would keep him safe.

On the night before his trial, an angel appeared in the prison cell and woke Peter up.

''Put on your shoes, wrap your cloak around you, and follow me,'' the angel said to Peter.

Peter could hardly believe what was happening! The chains fell off his wrists, doors opened and closed by a miracle, and he followed the angel out of the prison. Peter went to the house of his friends where they were amazed and overjoyed to see him safe.

But Herod was furious. He couldn't understand how Peter had escaped.

The unknown God

Years passed and Saul, now called Paul, had travelled to many different places to tell people about Jesus.

In Athens Paul was sad to see so many people worshipping idols and not knowing who God really was. He talked to anyone who would listen.

"I can see how much you want to please God," Paul said to them. "I even saw here an altar to an unknown God. But I can tell you that this God is not made of gold or silver or stone. He made the world and everything in it and made us to know him and to love him. God wants us to be sorry for all we have done wrong because one day Jesus, who died and came alive again, will come to judge us."

Some of the people there became Christians that day; others argued among themselves.

Paul is shipwrecked

Paul travelled many times by boat to tell others about Jesus. But toward the end of his life, Paul was taken to Rome as a prisoner .

While he was on a ship carrying 276 people, they ran into a terrible storm. But an angel appeared to Paul and told him that they would all arrive safely because God wanted him to arrive in Rome.

The boat was wrecked off the coast of Malta. Some of the passengers swam to the beach; others clung to the wreckage, but everyone on board reached the shore safely. No one was lost.

It was months before Paul arrived in Rome, and he stayed there in a house, with a soldier to guard him. Paul shared what he knew about Jesus as often as he could.

True love

Paul spent much of his time in Rome writing letters to Christians everywhere to help them live the way God wanted them to.

Paul taught them that they could show people how much they loved God by loving others.

''Love is patient, love is kind. Love is not greedy for other people's things. Love doesn't show off. Love is not proud or rude.

''Love always thinks of other people first. Love doesn't get angry too quickly. Love doesn't remind people of the bad things they've done.

''Love doesn't like to see nasty things. Love is always glad to hear what's right. Love always looks after people, always trusts, always hopes, always keeps on trying.

''Love never ends.''

Now there are followers of Jesus all over the world.

Stories can be found in the Bible as follows:

When the world began, Genesis 1:1 — 2:25

The whispering snake, Genesis 3:1-24

Noah's floating zoo, Genesis 6:5 — 9:17

Abraham moves house, Genesis 12:1— 13:18

A baby called laughter, Genesis 17:15 — 18:15,
   21:1-8

Jacob tricks his brother, Genesis 25:27-34, 27:1-45

Joseph, the favorite son, Genesis 37:1-36

A very happy family, Genesis 42:1 — 46:30

Miriam and the princess, Exodus 2:1-10

Flies, boils, and locusts, Exodus 5:1-2, 6:28 — 12:36

Escape from Egypt, Exodus 15:22 — 16:36

Ten rules for life, Exodus 20:1-17

The walls of Jericho, Joshua 5:13 — 6:27

Gideon's prayer, Judges 7:1-22

The boy who listened to God, 1 Samuel 3:1-21

David fights a giant, 1 Sam 17:1-54

The shepherd's song, Psalm 23

Solomon's special gift, 1 Kings 3:1-28

God looks after Elijah, 1 Kings 17:1-16

The little servant girl, 2 Kings 5:1-14

The one true God, Daniel 3:1-30

The lions' den, Daniel 6:1-28

Jonah runs away, Jonah 1:1 — 4:11

A baby born in Bethlehem, Luke 2:1-20

Gifts for the baby king, Matthew 2:1-12

John baptizes Jesus, Matthew 3:13-17

Jesus makes special friends, Matthew 4:18-22

God's blessing, Matthew 5:1-12

A prayer Jesus taught his friends,
   Matthew 6:5-15

The hole in the roof, Mark 2:1-12

The storm on the lake, Mark 4:35-41,
   Luke 8:23-27

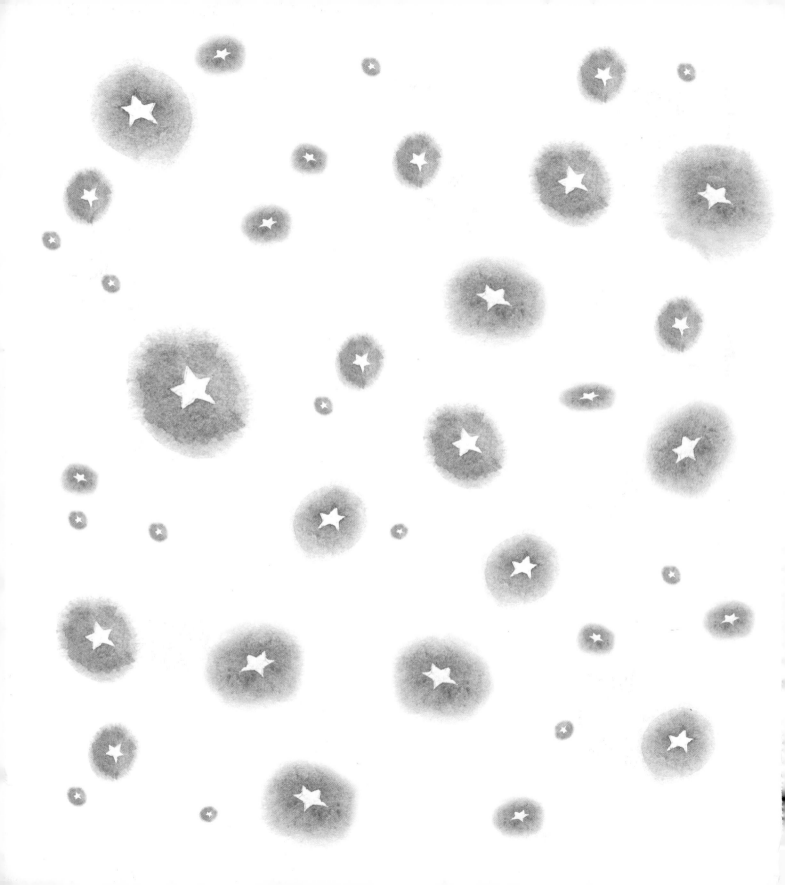